MASTERING LINKEDIN: A GUIDE TO WRITING ENGAGING POSTS

"Unlocking the Power of LinkedIn for Personal and Professional Success"

By

Chasity Bailey, JD, MA

and

Tomos Archer

ABOUT THE AUTHOR 162

INTRODUCTION

BACKGROUND ON THE IMPORTANCE OF LINKEDIN AS A PROFESSIONAL NETWORKING PLATFORM

LinkedIn has emerged as the premier professional networking platform, revolutionizing the way individuals connect, collaborate, and establish their online professional presence. With over 740 million users across more than 200 countries and territories, LinkedIn offers unparalleled opportunities to expand your professional network, showcase your expertise, and advance your career.

One of the key reasons why LinkedIn is so vital for professionals is its ability to connect individuals across industries, disciplines, and geographies. Unlike other social media platforms, LinkedIn is specifically designed for professional purposes, making it the go-to destination for forging valuable connections with like-minded professionals, colleagues, mentors, and potential employers.

LinkedIn provides a unique space for individuals to showcase their personal brand and establish thought leadership in their respective fields. Through posting engaging content, such as articles, videos, and updates, professionals can actively contribute to their industry's conversations and demonstrate their expertise. This opens up opportunities for collaboration, career growth, and even attracting new opportunities like job offers, partnerships, or speaking engagements.

In today's highly competitive job market, LinkedIn has become indispensable for job seekers and recruiters alike. Hiring managers and HR professionals often turn to LinkedIn to source candidates, review their profiles, and gain insights into their professional background and accomplishments. By maintaining an active and optimized LinkedIn profile, professionals increase their chances of being found by recruiters seeking talent.

Additionally, LinkedIn offers an array of features tailored to support professional development and learning. From industry-specific groups and forums to LinkedIn Learning courses and certifications, professionals can stay updated with the latest trends, expand their knowledge, and enhance their skill set.

Furthermore, LinkedIn has evolved into a platform where companies can establish a company presence, share updates about their products or services, and engage with their target audience. This presents an immense opportunity for professionals to connect with potential clients, showcase their work, and grow their business network.

In summary, LinkedIn has transformed the way professionals connect, communicate, and establish their personal brand. It serves as a powerful tool to expand professional networks, access new opportunities, and demonstrate expertise. Understanding the importance of LinkedIn as a professional networking platform is crucial for professionals looking to leverage its full potential and achieve professional success.

BENEFITS OF WRITING ENGAGING POSTS

Writing engaging LinkedIn posts can provide numerous benefits for professionals looking to establish their personal brand, build their network, and advance their career. Here are some key benefits of writing engaging LinkedIn posts:

Increased Visibility: Engaging posts have the potential to reach a wider audience on LinkedIn. When your posts receive high engagement - likes, comments, and shares - they tend to appear in the feed of other professionals, increasing your visibility and reach within your industry.

Thought Leadership: By sharing valuable insights, industry knowledge, and expertise through your posts, you position yourself as a thought leader in your field. Thought leaders are seen as knowledgeable and trustworthy, which can attract new connections, collaborations, job opportunities, and industry recognition.

Networking Opportunities: Engaging posts help you connect with like-minded professionals, industry peers, potential mentors, and even prospective employers or clients. By fostering conversations and building relationships through your posts, you expand your network and create opportunities for future collaborations and partnerships.

Personal Branding: LinkedIn is an excellent platform to establish and enhance your personal brand. Consistently writing engaging posts demonstrates your expertise, interests, and unique value proposition, shaping the way others perceive you professionally. Strong personal branding can open doors to new opportunities, such as speaking engagements, media interviews, or invitations to industry events.

Career Growth: Engaging LinkedIn posts can significantly impact your career growth. When you consistently share valuable and insightful content, you showcase your expertise to a wider audience and position yourself as a go-to professional in your field. This can lead to career advancement opportunities, job offers, or invitations to industry events or speaking engagements.

Knowledge Sharing: LinkedIn is a platform built for professionals to learn from each other. By sharing your experiences, insights, and lessons learned through your posts, you contribute to the collective knowledge of your industry. This not only establishes your credibility but also helps others grow and learn from your expertise.

Building Trust and Credibility: Writing engaging posts helps build trust and credibility among your network. When you consistently provide valuable content, engage in meaningful conversations, and demonstrate your expertise, others perceive you as knowledgeable, reliable, and trustworthy. This fosters stronger professional relationships and opens doors to collaborative opportunities.

Brand Promotion: Engaging posts also create opportunities to promote your personal brand or business. Whether you share updates about your work, achievements, projects, or events, LinkedIn posts allow you to showcase your brand and attract potential clients, customers, or partners.

In conclusion, writing engaging LinkedIn posts offers a range of benefits, including increased visibility, thought leadership, networking opportunities, personal branding, career growth, knowledge sharing, building trust, and brand promotion. Consistently creating valuable and engaging content on LinkedIn can significantly enhance your professional journey and open doors to new and exciting opportunities.

UNDERSTANDING LINKEDIN'S AUDIENCE

OVERVIEW OF LINKEDIN DEMOGRAPHICS AND USER BEHAVIOR

LinkedIn has a diverse user base, consisting primarily of professionals, job seekers, recruiters, and business-oriented individuals. Understanding the demographics and user behavior on LinkedIn can help you tailor your content and engage with your target audience effectively. Here is an overview of LinkedIn demographics and user behavior:

Professional Demographics:

LinkedIn is widely used in over 200 countries and territories, with more than 740 million users (as of October 2021).

The platform has a fairly even gender distribution, with slightly more male users than female.

LinkedIn is popular among professionals across various industries, including technology, finance, marketing, healthcare, consulting, and more.

The majority of LinkedIn users are college-educated, with many holding advanced degrees.

LinkedIn's user base spans a wide range of age groups, but the largest demographic is typically between 25-34 years old, closely followed by users in the 35-54 age range.

17

User Behavior and Engagement:

LinkedIn users are primarily focused on professional networking, career growth, and industry news.

Many users visit LinkedIn to explore job opportunities, search and apply for positions, and connect with potential employers or colleagues.

Compared to other social media platforms, LinkedIn users tend to spend more time engaging with professional content, such as industry articles, thought leadership posts, and business-related discussions.

User engagement on LinkedIn is often driven by educational and informative content that helps professionals enhance their skills, stay updated with industry trends, and solve work-related challenges.

Users actively engage with content through likes, comments, and shares, with conversations often revolving around professional interests, career advice, and industry insights.

LinkedIn users also participate in groups, where they can connect with other professionals in their industry or interest area, share knowledge, discuss industry topics, and seek advice.

Mobile Usage:

LinkedIn has a strong mobile presence, with a significant portion of users accessing the platform via the LinkedIn mobile app.

Users often use the mobile app to stay connected, engage with content on the go, and receive notifications for relevant updates, job opportunities, or messages.

LinkedIn Premium Subscriptions:

LinkedIn offers premium subscription plans, such as LinkedIn Premium and Sales Navigator, which provide additional features and benefits.

Premium subscribers have access to enhanced search options, expanded profile visibility, InMail messaging to connect with professionals outside their network, and analytics to track post performance.

Understanding the demographics and user behavior on LinkedIn can help you tailor your content, networking, and engagement strategies to effectively connect and engage with your target audience. By aligning your efforts with the preferences and interests of LinkedIn users, you can maximize the impact of your professional presence on the platform.

IDENTIFYING YOUR TARGET AUDIENCE AND THEIR INTERESTS

To effectively reach and engage your target audience on LinkedIn, it's crucial to identify who they are and understand their interests. Here are some steps to help you identify your target audience and their interests:

Define Your Objective: Clearly outline your goals and what you aim to achieve on LinkedIn. Are you looking to connect with industry professionals, attract potential clients, or position yourself as a thought leader? Defining your objectives will shape your target audience and the content you create.

Research Your Industry: Conduct thorough research on your industry to gain insights into its trends, challenges, and key players. Identify the demographics and characteristics of professionals in your field, such as job titles, industries, company sizes, and geographic locations.

Analyze Your Current Network: Review your existing LinkedIn connections and assess their relevance to your goals. Look for patterns in their industries, roles, and interests. This analysis can help you identify commonalities and refine your target audience.

Ideal Client or Audience Persona: Create an ideal client persona or audience persona that represents your ideal target audience. Consider factors such as job title, industry, educational background, skills, interests, and challenges. This persona will guide your content creation and engagement strategies.

LinkedIn Search Functions: Utilize LinkedIn's search functions to find professionals or companies that align with your target audience. Use filters like industry, location, keywords, and connections to refine your search results. Explore the profiles and content of individuals you find to gain further insights into their interests and preferences.

Engage and Survey: Engage with your target audience by participating in groups, contributing to discussions, and commenting on relevant posts. This will not only help you establish connections but also provide an opportunity to learn more about their interests and challenges. You can also consider conducting surveys or polls on LinkedIn to gather specific insights from your target audience.

Analyze Your Content Performance: Monitor the performance of your LinkedIn posts to understand which types of content resonate the most with your target audience. Track metrics such as likes, comments, shares, and views to identify the topics, formats, and styles that generate the highest engagement. This data will help you refine your content strategy and address the interests of your audience.

Stay Updated with Industry News: Regularly read industry publications, blogs, and forums to stay informed about the latest trends and topics in your field. By staying updated, you can create content that addresses current discussions and interests within your industry.

Remember, identifying your target audience is an ongoing process. Continuously monitor and adapt your strategies to align with evolving trends and preferences. By understanding your target audience's interests, you can create content that resonates with them, establish meaningful connections, and achieve your LinkedIn goals.

HOW TO TAILOR YOUR POSTS FOR MAXIMUM ENGAGEMENT

To tailor your LinkedIn posts for maximum engagement, consider the following tips:

Understand Your Audience: Know your target audience's interests, needs, and pain points. This understanding will help you create content that resonates with them and drives engagement.

Choose Compelling Headlines: Craft attention-grabbing headlines that pique curiosity or address a specific problem. Use compelling language, numbers, or intriguing statements to entice readers to click and read more.

Use Visuals Strategically: Incorporate eye-catching visuals, such as high-quality images, infographics, or videos, to make your posts visually appealing and engaging. Visuals can help convey information quickly and increase the likelihood of capturing readers' attention.

Write Concise and Scannable Content: LinkedIn users often quickly skim through posts, so make your content easy to read and understand. Break down paragraphs into shorter sentences, use headings or bullet points, and highlight key takeaways to make it scannable.

Provide Value and Insights: Share valuable insights, tips, or industry knowledge in your posts. Offering helpful information will position you as an expert and motivate readers to engage with your content by liking, commenting, or sharing.

Spark Engagement with Questions or Calls to Action: Encourage interaction by ending your posts with thought-provoking questions or clear calls to action. This prompts readers to leave comments, share their opinions or experiences, or engage in meaningful conversations.

Personalize and Humanize: Make your posts more relatable and personal by sharing anecdotes, personal experiences, or storytelling elements. This humanizes your content and helps create a connection with your audience.

Use Relevant Hashtags: Research and include relevant industry-specific hashtags in your posts. This increases the discoverability of your content and allows others interested in those topics to find and engage with your post.

Engage Responsively: Respond promptly and thoughtfully to comments on your posts. Engaging with your audience shows that you value their input and encourages further interaction.

Analyze and Optimize: Regularly review the performance of your posts using LinkedIn analytics. Identify patterns, content types, or topics that generate higher engagement and adjust your content strategy accordingly.

Experiment and Adapt: Don't be afraid to experiment with different formats, topics, or styles of posts to discover what works best for your audience. Be open to feedback and adapt your content accordingly to improve engagement over time.

Remember, building engagement takes time and consistent effort. By delivering valuable content, sparking conversations, and actively engaging with your audience, you can maximize the engagement on your LinkedIn posts.

CRAFTING ATTENTION-GRABBING HEADLINES

IMPORTANCE OF STRONG HEADLINES TO ATTRACT VIEWERS

Strong headlines play a crucial role in attracting viewers and capturing their attention on LinkedIn. Here are some key reasons highlighting the importance of strong headlines:

Grab Attention: In a fast-paced online world, attention spans are short. A strong headline is essential to immediately grab the attention of LinkedIn users as they scroll through their feed. It needs to be compelling, intriguing, and stand out among the sea of other content.

Increase Click-through Rates: A strong headline entices viewers to click on your post to read more. The headline serves as a preview of the content and should effectively communicate the value or benefit they will gain from engaging with your post. Higher click-through rates result in more people engaging with your content and potentially expanding your reach.

Improve Visibility: LinkedIn's algorithm takes into account engagement metrics like clicks, likes, and comments to determine the visibility of a post. A strong headline can significantly increase the chances of your post being clicked on and engaged with, boosting its visibility in users' feeds and increasing the likelihood of reaching a larger audience.

Establish Relevance: A well-crafted headline quickly communicates what your post is about, establishing relevance and helping viewers understand why they should invest their time in reading it. It should align with the interests and needs of your target audience, signaling that your content is valuable and worth their attention.

Encourage Social Sharing: Compelling headlines make it more likely for viewers to share your post with their network. When your content is shared, it reaches a wider audience, potentially leading to increased engagement, new connections, and broader visibility for your personal brand or business.

Boost Brand Perception: Strong headlines contribute to establishing a positive brand impression. When your headlines consistently deliver valuable, insightful, or thought-provoking content, viewers associate your brand with expertise, credibility, and quality. This builds trust and encourages viewers to engage with future content.

Differentiate from Competitors: LinkedIn is a competitive platform with numerous professionals vying for attention. By creating strong headlines, you differentiate yourself from your competitors and stand out as someone worth paying attention to. Through unique phrasing, powerful words, or intriguing questions, you can capture viewers' interest and compel them to engage with your content.

Remember, a strong headline is just the beginning. Ensure that your content delivers on the promise made in the headline and provides value to the viewers. By consistently creating engaging content with strong headlines, you can maximize your impact on LinkedIn and attract a larger, more engaged audience.

TECHNIQUES FOR WRITING HEADLINES

Writing compelling headlines is essential for capturing the attention of viewers on LinkedIn. Here are some techniques to help you craft engaging and compelling headlines:

Be Clear and Concise: Use clear and concise language to communicate the main benefit or takeaway of your post. Avoid ambiguity or jargon that may confuse readers. Make sure your headline can be easily understood and quickly captures the essence of your content.

Create a Sense of Urgency: Incorporate words or phrases that create a sense of urgency, such as "Now," "Limited Time," or "Don't Miss Out." This encourages viewers to take immediate action and engage with your post.

Use Numbers and Data: Including numbers in your headline can make it more attention-grabbing and provide a tangible promise of what readers will gain from your content. For example, "5 Strategies for Boosting Your LinkedIn Engagement" or "Increase Your Network by 30% with These Tips."

Pose a Question: Asking a question in your headline can pique curiosity and engage viewers by inviting them to reflect or seek an answer. Make sure the question is relevant and addresses a problem or challenge your audience may have. Example: "Struggling to Write Engaging LinkedIn Posts?

Here's What You Need to Know."

Use Power Words: Employ impactful and persuasive words that evoke emotion and capture attention. Power words like "proven," "exclusive," "ultimate," "essential," or "secret" can add a sense of value and intrigue to your headline.

Demonstrate Value or Benefits: Clearly communicate the value or benefits readers will gain from engaging with your post. Whether it's knowledge, insights, solutions, or inspiration, emphasize what they stand to gain by clicking on your content.

Create a How-To or Guide: Frame your headline as a step-by-step guide or a how-to resource. This signals that your post provides practical advice or solutions to a specific problem, making it more enticing for viewers to click and read more.

Tailor to Your Target Audience: Consider the interests, needs, and pain points of your target audience and incorporate relevant keywords or phrases in your headline. Speak directly to their challenges or aspirations to make the headline more relatable and compelling.

Use Emotional Triggers: Tap into emotions by using words or phrases that trigger curiosity, excitement, or a desire for self-improvement. Emotionally engaging headlines tend to capture attention and evoke a response from viewers.

Test and Refine: Experiment with different headline variations to see which ones resonate best with your audience. Monitor engagement metrics, such as click-through rates or comments, and refine your approach based on the results.

Remember, while headlines are important, ensure that the content of your post delivers on the promise and provides value to the audience. By using these techniques and refining your approach over time, you can create compelling headlines that capture attention and drive engagement on LinkedIn.

DOS AND DON'TS FOR LINKEDIN POSTS

Dos for LinkedIn post headlines:

Do be clear and concise: Make sure your headline clearly communicates the main point or benefit of your post in a concise manner.

Do use keywords: Incorporate relevant keywords that resonate with your target audience and enhance the visibility of your post on LinkedIn's search results.

Do be specific: Provide specific details or numbers in your headline to create a clear and specific promise of what readers will gain by engaging with your content.

Do create curiosity: Use intriguing or thought-provoking language to generate curiosity and make viewers curious to click on your post to learn more.

Do tailor to your audience: Understand your target audience and customize your headline to address their interests, challenges, or aspirations. This helps in making your headline more relatable and engaging.

Do align with your content: Ensure that your headline accurately represents the content of your post and delivers on the promise made in the headline. This helps in building trust and credibility with your audience.

Do test and iterate: Experiment with different headline variations and monitor their performance. Analyze engagement metrics to identify which headlines resonate best with your audience and iterate accordingly.

Don'ts for LinkedIn post headlines:

Don't overpromise: Avoid using hyperbolic language that may overpromise the value of your content. Be honest and realistic about what readers can expect from your post.

Don't be vague or generic: Stay away from generic or vague headlines that don't clearly indicate the content or value of your post. Ambiguous headlines may fail to capture viewers' attention and result in low engagement.

Don't use clickbait tactics: While it's important to create curiosity, refrain from using misleading or deceptive clickbait tactics. Misrepresenting the content with sensationalized headlines can damage your credibility and trust with your audience.

Don't use excessive jargon: Avoid using industry jargon or complex vocabulary that may confuse or alienate your audience. Use language that is easily understood and relatable to your target audience.

Don't make it too long: Keep your headline concise and attention-grabbing. Lengthy headlines can get cut off in users' feeds, resulting in decreased visibility and lower engagement.

Don't neglect proofreading: Ensure that your headline is free from spelling or grammatical errors. Poorly written headlines can create a negative impression and undermine the quality of your content.

Don't rely solely on headlines: While headlines are important, remember that the content of your post is equally crucial. Ensure that your content delivers on the promise made in the headline and provides value to your audience.

By following these dos and don'ts, you can create effective and engaging headlines that captivate your audience's attention and drive higher engagement on your LinkedIn posts.

STRUCTURING YOUR LINKEDIN POSTS

Ideal length for LinkedIn posts

The ideal length for LinkedIn posts can vary depending on the type of content and your specific goals. While LinkedIn allows posts of up to 1,300 characters, research and best practices suggest that shorter posts tend to perform better in terms of engagement. Here are some guidelines to consider:

Short and Snappy: Keep your LinkedIn posts concise and to the point. Aim for posts that are between 150-300 characters in length. Shorter posts are easier to read and digest, especially considering that LinkedIn users often browse through their feed quickly.

Use Teasers for Longer-Form Content: If you have longer-form content, such as an article or blog post, you can create a teaser in your LinkedIn post with a brief summary or compelling snippet. Then, provide a link or prompt viewers to click through to read the full article on a website or blog.

Break Down Longer Content: If you have more to say in your LinkedIn post, consider breaking it down into shorter paragraphs or bullet points. This helps to make the content more scannable and digestible for readers.

Prioritize Value and Conciseness: Regardless of the length, focus on delivering value and capturing attention in your LinkedIn posts. Use impactful language, share actionable insights, and clearly communicate the key takeaways. Make every word count.

Experiment and Observe: Test different lengths for your LinkedIn posts and observe the engagement metrics to determine what resonates best with your audience. Pay attention to likes, comments, and shares to identify patterns and adjust your content strategy accordingly.

Remember, while shorter posts generally tend to perform well, it's important to be flexible and adapt to your specific audience and content. Monitor the engagement and feedback from your LinkedIn posts to determine the optimal length that resonates with your target audience and serves your goals effectively.

INTRODUCTION TO THE INVERTED PYRAMID STRUCTURE

The inverted pyramid structure is a writing technique commonly used in journalism and content creation. It involves organizing information in a specific order, starting with the most important and essential details at the beginning, followed by supporting details, and ending with additional background or less critical information. This structure is named "inverted" because it flips the traditional pyramid, where the broadest information is at the top and gradually narrows down.

The purpose of using the inverted pyramid structure is to immediately capture the reader's attention and provide them with the most crucial information upfront. This approach acknowledges the reality that readers often skim or have limited time, so it ensures that they can quickly grasp the core message or key takeaways without having to read the entire piece.

In the context of writing a LinkedIn post, adopting the inverted pyramid structure can help you effectively communicate your main points and engage your audience. By presenting the key message or most important details at the beginning of your post, you immediately capture interest and provide value to the reader. This approach is particularly useful when you want to share news, insights, or actionable tips in a concise and engaging manner.

Following the inverted pyramid structure in your LinkedIn post allows your audience to quickly understand the main points even if they only read the beginning or skim through the content. It also helps to actively engage your readers and encourage them to continue reading or engage further by asking questions, seeking their thoughts or opinions, or inviting them to take specific actions.

In summary, the inverted pyramid structure is an effective way to structure your LinkedIn posts by presenting the most important details at the beginning, followed by supporting information. By adopting this approach, you can instantly grab the attention of your audience, provide immediate value, and ensure your message is effectively communicated even if readers only engage with the beginning of your post.

BREAKING DOWN CONTENT INTO SECTIONS FOR READABILITY

Breaking down content into sections is an effective technique for enhancing readability and making your LinkedIn posts more accessible and engaging to readers. Here are some tips on how to break down content into sections:

Use Headings and Subheadings: Headings and subheadings help organize your content and provide visual cues to guide readers through your post. Use clear, descriptive headings to introduce each section or key point. This helps readers quickly scan the post and find the information they are interested in.

Keep Paragraphs Short: Lengthy paragraphs can be overwhelming and make it difficult for readers to consume your content. Aim for paragraphs that are 2-3 sentences long. Short paragraphs are easier to read, and the white space around them improves overall readability.

Utilize Bulleted or Numbered Lists: When presenting a series of related points or steps, use bulleted or numbered lists. Lists make the information more digestible, visually appealing, and easier to skim. They also help readers understand and remember the main points more effectively.

Break Content with Visual Elements: Incorporate visual elements, such as relevant images, infographics, or pull quotes, to break up text-heavy sections. These visuals provide a visual break and grab readers' attention, enhancing overall readability.

Highlight Key Information: Use bold, italics, or other formatting options to highlight important keywords, phrases, or quotes. This emphasizes the essential elements and helps readers quickly understand the main points or takeaways from your content.

Provide Subheadings within Sections: If a section of your post covers multiple related points, consider using subheadings within that section. Subheadings provide structure and make it easier for readers to navigate and comprehend specific aspects of your content.

Ensure Logical Flow: Ensure that your content flows logically from one section to the next. Each section should build on the previous one and contribute to the overall coherence and clarity of your post.

Consider Using Pull Quotes or Callout Boxes: Pull quotes or callout boxes are visually distinct elements that highlight a particularly impactful or insightful statement from your post. These elements capture attention and reinforce key messages.

By breaking down your content into sections, incorporating headings, utilizing lists, and adding visual elements, you make your LinkedIn posts easier to read and navigate. This improves readability, encourages engagement, and enhances the overall user experience for your audience.

HASHTAGS

The optimal number of hashtags to use in a LinkedIn post can vary. LinkedIn allows a maximum of 30 hashtags per post, but it doesn't mean you should always use the maximum. Here are some guidelines to consider:

Relevant and Specific: Focus on using hashtags that are relevant to your post's content and target audience. Choose specific keywords or phrases that accurately describe the main theme or topic of your post.

Quality over Quantity: Rather than stuffing your post with a large number of hashtags, prioritize using a smaller number of high-quality hashtags that are most likely to resonate with your target audience. Aim for a balanced mix of popular and niche hashtags.

3-5 Hashtags: In general, using 3-5 hashtags generates better engagement on LinkedIn. This allows you to maintain post readability and clarity while still benefiting from hashtag reach.

Mix Broad and Specific Hashtags: Include a combination of broader industry-related hashtags and more specific hashtags that target your niche or topic. This approach helps you reach a wider audience while also reaching those specifically interested in your post's content.

Customize for Each Post: Tailor your hashtag selection for each individual post. Consider the specific topic, target audience, and relevant keywords to find the most appropriate and effective hashtags for each piece of content.

Monitor Performance: Track the performance of your posts with different hashtags using LinkedIn's analytics tools. This will help you identify which hashtags are generating the most engagement and adjust your hashtag strategy accordingly.

Remember, the use of hashtags on LinkedIn is not as widespread as on other social media platforms like Instagram or Twitter. Therefore, choosing a smaller number of high-quality, relevant hashtags is generally more effective in reaching your desired audience and sparking meaningful discussions.

STORYTELLING TECHNIQUES

IMPORTANCE OF STORYTELLING ON LINKEDIN

Storytelling plays a paramount role in LinkedIn posts as it helps to captivate, engage, and connect with your audience on a deeper level. Here are some key reasons highlighting the importance of storytelling in LinkedIn posts:

Grabbing Attention: Well-crafted stories have the power to capture the attention of your audience right from the start. Stories evoke curiosity and curiosity prompts readers to continue reading, allowing you to make an immediate impact with your content.

Building Emotional Connection: Stories have the ability to evoke emotions and create a personal connection with your audience. By sharing relatable experiences, challenges, or triumphs, you establish a human connection that resonates with readers and makes your content more memorable.

Enhancing Memorability: Facts and figures alone can be forgettable, but stories create lasting impressions. When you weave information or insights into a narrative, it becomes more memorable and relatable for your audience. This increases the chances that they will remember and refer back to your post in the future.

Demonstrating Expertise: Storytelling allows you to showcase your expertise by providing real-life examples, case studies, or personal anecdotes. Your ability to narrate relevant stories demonstrates your knowledge, experience, and credibility in a way that mere statements or self-promotion cannot.

Fostering Engagement: Engaging stories prompt readers to engage with your content by liking, commenting, or sharing their own experiences. Stories have an inherent way of stimulating conversations, generating feedback, and fostering connections within your LinkedIn community.

Inspiring Action: Stories can be inspirational and motivational, encouraging your audience to take action or apply lessons in their own lives or professional endeavors. A well-told story can prompt readers to make positive changes, pursue new opportunities, or adopt different perspectives.

Differentiating Yourself: LinkedIn is a platform filled with professionals sharing insights and knowledge. By incorporating storytelling, you can differentiate yourself from others by adding a unique and personal touch to your content. Your stories help you stand out and create a distinct voice that draws readers in.

Creating Brand Identity: Stories contribute to building your personal or professional brand identity on LinkedIn. Consistently sharing engaging and authentic stories helps shape how others perceive you and reinforces your values, expertise, and passions.

By incorporating storytelling into your LinkedIn posts, you can captivate your audience, establish a stronger connection, demonstrate expertise, foster engagement, and enhance your overall brand presence. Stories have the power to leave a lasting impact and make your content more meaningful and memorable in the minds of your readers.

HOW TO FIND AND DEVELOP PERSONAL OR PROFESSIONAL STORIES

Finding and developing personal or professional stories for your LinkedIn posts can help you connect with your audience on a deeper level and make your content more engaging. Here are some steps to help you find and develop compelling stories:

Reflect on Your Experiences: Begin by reflecting on your personal or professional journey. Think about significant milestones, challenges you've overcome, achievements, or lessons learned along the way. Consider experiences that have shaped your perspective, skills, or values.

Identify Relevant Themes: Look for common themes or topics that align with your professional goals, expertise, or the interests of your target audience. Focus on stories that are relevant and valuable to your audience, providing insights, solutions, or inspiration in areas they care about.

Choose the Right Angle: Determine the angle or message you want to convey through your story. Consider what you want your audience to take away or how you want to inspire or educate them. Have a clear purpose in mind before developing your narrative.

Craft a Compelling Structure: Structure your story with a clear beginning, middle, and end. Start by setting the context and introducing the main characters or factors involved. Then, develop the narrative, highlighting key challenges, turning points, or impactful moments. Finally, wrap up the story with a resolution, takeaway, or call for action.

Be Authentic and Genuine: Authenticity is crucial in storytelling. Share stories that are true to your experiences, values, and personality. Genuine stories resonate with your audience and build trust.

Use Vivid Language and Descriptions: Make your story come alive by using vivid language and sensory details. Paint a picture with your words, capturing the emotions, sensory experiences, and environments within your story.

Inject Emotion and Personal Connection: Emotions are a powerful storytelling tool. Infuse relatable emotions into your stories to make them more compelling and resonate with your audience on a deeper level. Allow your audience to connect with your experiences by conveying your own feelings and reactions.

Focus on Lessons Learned or Insights: Each story should have a key takeaway, lesson, or insight that is valuable to your audience. Clearly communicate this in your storytelling, providing tangible advice, strategies, or reflections that readers can apply in their own lives or professions.

Revise and Edit: Refine your story by revising and editing your content. Eliminate unnecessary details, streamline your narrative, and ensure clarity and coherence. Polish your language and structure to create a polished and impactful story.

Share with Authenticity and Purpose: When sharing your story on LinkedIn, be authentic and make a personal connection with your audience. Explain why this story is important to you and how it relates to your professional journey or industry. Clearly articulate the value or relevance of your story to your audience.

By following these steps, you can find and develop personal or professional stories that resonate with your audience, demonstrate your expertise, and create a meaningful connection on LinkedIn. Remember, storytelling is a powerful tool, so leverage it to share experiences, inspire others, and build a strong professional network.

TIPS FOR ENGAGING STORYTELLING ON LINKEDIN

Engaging storytelling on LinkedIn can captivate your audience and make your content more compelling. Here are some tips to help you create engaging storytelling on LinkedIn:

Know Your Audience: Understand the interests, needs, and preferences of your target audience on LinkedIn. Tailor your storytelling approach to resonate with their aspirations, challenges, or professional goals.

Start with a Hook: Begin your storytelling with a hook that grabs the reader's attention right from the start. Use an intriguing statement, a thought-provoking question, or a captivating anecdote to draw readers in and compel them to continue reading.

Show, Don't Just Tell: Use descriptive language and vivid details to immerse your readers in the story. Paint a picture with your words, allowing readers to visualize the scenes, emotions, or experiences you are describing.

Create Relatable Characters: Whether you are telling a personal story or illustrating a professional scenario, develop relatable characters to make your storytelling more engaging. These characters could be based on real individuals, archetypes, or representations of common experiences.

Build Suspense and Tension: Engaging storytelling often involves creating suspense or tension. Add elements of conflict, obstacles, or challenges to your narrative, keeping readers intrigued and eager to know how the story unfolds.

Use Dialogue: Incorporate dialogue to bring your story to life. By using direct quotes or conversations, you create a more dynamic and interactive narrative that engages readers on a deeper level.

Make it Authentic and Personal: Authenticity is key to captivating storytelling. Share personal experiences, vulnerabilities, or lessons learned to create a genuine connection with your audience. Be open and honest, allowing readers to relate to your journey.

Focus on Emotions and Values: Tap into emotions to make your storytelling more impactful. Identify the emotions within your story and convey them effectively to create empathy, resonance, or inspire action. Additionally, highlight the values or principles that underpin your story to reinforce your message.

Incorporate Visuals: Visual elements, such as relevant images, infographics, or videos, can enhance your storytelling on LinkedIn. Visuals add another layer of engagement, helping to convey your story and evoke emotions more effectively.

Have a Clear Message or Takeaway: Ensure your storytelling has a clear message, lesson, or takeaway that is valuable to your audience. Drive home the purpose of your story and provide insights or actionable steps that readers can apply in their own lives or professions.

Encourage Engagement: Prompt readers to engage with your storytelling by asking relevant questions, inviting them to share their own experiences or insights, or encouraging them to take specific actions. This encourages meaningful conversations and builds a sense of community around your content.

Revise and Refine: Edit your storytelling to ensure it flows smoothly, maintains reader engagement, and is concise. Pay attention to the pacing, clarity, and overall impact of your narrative. Revise and refine your content to make it as engaging as possible.

Remember, the key to engaging storytelling on LinkedIn is capturing the attention and emotions of your audience. By crafting compelling narratives, providing value, and creating a sense of connection, you can create engaging stories that captivate your audience and foster meaningful engagement on the platform.

VISUALS AND MULTIMEDIA

TYPES OF VISUALS THAT WORK ON LINKEDIN

LinkedIn is a professional networking platform that emphasizes informative and visually appealing content. Various types of visuals work well on LinkedIn, providing an engaging and impactful way to convey information. Here are some types of visuals that work effectively on LinkedIn:

Professional Headshots: A high-quality headshot can help you make a strong first impression on LinkedIn. It serves as a visual representation of your professional identity and helps establish credibility.

Infographics: Infographics condense complex information into visually appealing and easy-to-understand graphics. They are great for presenting statistics, data, or step-by-step processes in a concise and visually engaging manner.

Images and Photos: Incorporating relevant and high-resolution images or photos in your LinkedIn posts can increase visual appeal and capture the attention of your audience. Use images that align with your content and help convey your message effectively.

Videos: LinkedIn supports native video uploads, making it a powerful platform for sharing video content. Videos can be used to deliver presentations, share industry insights, provide tutorial demonstrations, or share stories. They are highly engaging and can effectively communicate complex concepts in an easily digestible format.

Slide Presentations: LinkedIn's SlideShare feature allows you to upload and share slide presentations. Slide presentations are effective for showcasing expertise, providing educational content, or presenting visual narratives that can be easily navigated.

Charts and Graphs: Incorporating charts and graphs is a great way to visually represent data or trends, especially when discussing industry insights, market research, or performance metrics. Clear and well-designed charts can quickly communicate important information to your audience.

Visual Quotes: Sharing visually appealing quotes related to your industry or expertise can capture attention and resonate with your audience. Use design tools to create visually striking quote images that prominently display your message.

Screenshots: When sharing insights or discussing digital tools or platforms, screenshots can be highly valuable. They provide concrete examples and make it easier for your audience to understand specific features or processes related to your topic.

Interactive Content: LinkedIn also supports interactive content formats like interactive images or surveys. These types of visuals allow your audience to actively engage and participate with your content, increasing their involvement and interest.

Remember, when using visuals on LinkedIn, it's important to ensure they are professional, relevant, and add value to your content. Visuals should enhance the information you're sharing and align with your personal or professional brand. Experiment with different types of visuals to determine what resonates best with your audience and supports your storytelling goals on LinkedIn.

USING IMAGES, INFOGRAPHICS, AND VIDEOS EFFECTIVELY

Using images, infographics, and videos effectively on LinkedIn can enhance the visual appeal of your content and engage your audience. Here are some tips for using these visuals effectively:

Choose High-Quality Visuals: Ensure that the images, infographics, or videos you use are of high quality and resolution. Blurry or low-quality visuals can detract from the overall impact of your content. Use clear, well-composed images and videos that align with your message and brand.

Align Visuals with Content: Make sure your visuals directly relate to the content and add value to your message. Whether it's an image, infographic, or video, it should enhance the understanding or impact of your text-based content, providing context or supporting information.

Create Engaging Thumbnails or Previews: For videos, choose an enticing thumbnail or preview image that captures attention and encourages viewers to click and watch. The visual preview should give viewers an idea of what to expect and compel them to engage with your video content.

Keep Visuals Concise and Clear: Ensure that your visuals are easily comprehensible and don't overwhelm the viewer. Use simple and clear designs, labels, or captions that convey the intended information effectively. Infographics should present information in a visually organized and digestible format.

Add Captions or Descriptions: Include brief captions or descriptions for your visuals to provide context and clarity. This helps viewers understand the purpose or key points of the visual even if they don't read the accompanying text.

Incorporate Branding Elements: Consider adding your brand logo, colors, or other visual branding elements to your images, infographics, or videos. This helps reinforce your brand identity and create a consistent visual presence across your LinkedIn content.

Optimize for Mobile Viewing: The majority of LinkedIn users access the platform on mobile devices, so ensure that your visuals are optimized for mobile viewing. Test the size, formatting, and overall display of your visuals on mobile devices to ensure they appear as intended.

Encourage Interaction with Visuals: Prompt viewers to engage with your visuals by including a clear call to action. This could be asking viewers to comment, share, like, or take specific actions related to the visual content. Engaging visuals can spark conversations and encourage interaction with your LinkedIn posts.

Leverage LinkedIn Native Video: When using videos, consider uploading them directly to LinkedIn rather than sharing external links. Native videos have higher visibility, autoplay capabilities, and can generate higher engagement compared to external video links.

Test and Analyze: Experiment with different types of visuals, formats, or lengths, and analyze the performance of your posts. Monitor engagement metrics such as views, likes, comments, and shares to understand what resonates best with your audience. Use this data to refine your visual content strategy over time.

By using images, infographics, and videos effectively, you can capture attention, convey information more impactfully, and create engaging experiences for your LinkedIn audience. Remember to align your visuals with your content, optimize them for mobile viewing, and incorporate clear calls to action to encourage interaction and engagement.

BEST PRACTICES FOR VISUAL STORYTELLING ON THE PLATFORM

Visual storytelling on LinkedIn can be a powerful tool to engage your audience and convey your message effectively. Here are some best practices for visual storytelling on the platform:

Start with a Strong Visual Hook: Grab your audience's attention right away with a visually striking or intriguing image or video thumbnail. This will entice viewers to stop scrolling and explore your content.

Use Imagery that Supports Your Narrative: Select visuals that align with your story and enhance its impact. Whether it's a photo, infographic, or video snippet, ensure it effectively conveys the emotions, concepts, or themes you want to convey.

Keep it Relevant and Professional: Choose visuals that are relevant to your industry, topic, or message. Maintain a professional tone and aesthetic that aligns with the LinkedIn platform's standards.

Be Consistent with Branding: Utilize your brand colors, typography, and logo in your visual storytelling. Consistency in visual branding creates recognition and reinforces your professional brand identity.

Use Captions and Descriptions: Include concise and compelling captions or descriptions that provide context and enhance understanding. Use captions to reinforce your message or create intrigue that encourages viewers to engage further.

Infuse Key Data or Statistics: If applicable, incorporate data or statistics into your visual storytelling to support your narrative and add credibility. Displaying relevant information visually can enhance comprehension and deliver a memorable impact.

Maintain Visual Cohesion: Ensure that your visuals flow cohesively from one to the next. Use consistent styles, color schemes, or themes to create a visually appealing and unified narrative.

Choose the Right Format and Length: Consider the most suitable format and length for your visual storytelling. Choose between images, infographics, or videos based on the nature of your content and your audience's preferences. Tailor the length to match the attention span and engagement habits of LinkedIn users.

Incorporate Subtitles or Graphics for Videos: Since videos on LinkedIn often autoplay without sound, include subtitles or graphics that convey key messages or highlights. This allows viewers to understand the content even when watching on mute.

Encourage Engagement and Call to Action: Prompt viewers to engage with your visual content by including a clear call to action in your captions or accompanying text. Ask questions, invite comments, or encourage sharing to stimulate interaction with your audience.

Test and Analyze Performance: Monitor the engagement metrics of your visual storytelling, including likes, comments, shares, and click-through rates. Analyze the performance data to understand what resonates best with your audience and refine your visual storytelling strategy.

By applying these best practices, you can effectively engage your audience, communicate your message, and strengthen your professional presence through impactful visual storytelling on LinkedIn.

ADDING VALUE WITH DATA AND INSIGHTS

USING STATISTICS, SURVEYS, AND RESEARCH TO SUPPORT YOUR POINTS

Using statistics, surveys, and research to support your points on LinkedIn can add credibility, strengthen your arguments, and enhance the value of your content. Here are some best practices for incorporating data into your LinkedIn posts:

Use Reliable Sources: Ensure you gather data from reputable and reliable sources. Use data from respected organizations, industry reports, academic studies, or reputable publications. This helps establish the credibility of the information you're sharing.

Select Relevant and Recent Data: Choose data that is relevant to your topic, audience, and the points you are making. Select recent data whenever possible to ensure the information is up to date and reflects current trends or insights in your industry.

Present Data in an Engaging Format: Consider using eye-catching visuals such as charts, graphs, or infographics to present your data. Visual representations make data more digestible and increase its impact, making it easier for readers to understand and remember.

Provide Context and Interpretation: When sharing data, it's crucial to provide context and interpret the findings. Explain what the data means, why it is important, and how it supports your point or argument. Help your audience understand the implications or conclusions that can be drawn from the data.

Keep it Concise and Focused: Avoid overwhelming your audience with excessive data. Select the most relevant and impactful statistics or research findings that directly support your main points. Keep your data-focused statements concise and ensure they align with the broader message of your content.

Attribute Your Sources: Give credit to the original sources of the data to maintain transparency and demonstrate your adherence to intellectual property rights. Provide proper citations or links to the source material whenever possible.

Use Data to Tell a Story: Weave data into your storytelling to make it more compelling and relatable. Integrate data points as evidence to support anecdotes, personal experiences, or industry insights, creating a narrative that resonates with your audience.

Balance Data with Practical Application: While data is valuable, balance it with real-world examples or practical applications. Help your audience understand how the data translates into action or how it can be applied to their professional lives or industry.

Encourage Discussion and Debate: Prompt your audience to engage by inviting them to share their thoughts, experiences, or opinions related to the data you have shared. Encourage them to contribute to the conversation and provide their own perspectives on the topic.

Update Data Over Time: As new data becomes available or as statistics change, update your content accordingly. Keeping your data fresh and relevant helps maintain the accuracy and timeliness of your arguments or insights.

By incorporating statistics, surveys, and research into your LinkedIn posts effectively, you can enhance the credibility of your content, support your arguments, and provide valuable insights to your audience. This strengthens your professional presence and positions you as an informed and authoritative voice within your industry.

IMPORTANCE OF PROVIDING VALUABLE INSIGHTS TO READERS

Providing valuable insights to readers on LinkedIn is crucial for establishing credibility, building trust, and positioning yourself as a knowledgeable professional in your field. Here are some reasons highlighting the importance of providing valuable insights:

Demonstrating Expertise: Sharing valuable insights showcases your expertise and deep understanding of your industry or profession. It positions you as a thought leader and someone who is knowledgeable about current trends, best practices, and emerging opportunities.

Building Trust and Credibility: When you consistently provide valuable insights, your audience begins to trust your expertise and rely on your content for reliable information. This trust helps establish your credibility and fosters stronger connections and professional relationships.

Establishing Your Unique Voice: Providing valuable insights allows you to differentiate yourself from others in your industry. By sharing unique perspectives, original research, or innovative ideas, you shape your professional brand and create a distinct voice that sets you apart from the crowd.

Adding Practical Value: Valuable insights offer tangible benefits to your audience. Whether it's sharing tips, strategies, or industry-specific knowledge, you provide practical value that readers can apply to their own professional lives. This helps them solve problems, improve their skills, or gain new perspectives.

Fostering Engagement and Discussion: Valuable insights often prompt your audience to engage with your content. They may leave comments, ask questions, or share their own experiences and opinions. This interaction creates a sense of community and encourages meaningful discussions, expanding your network and deepening professional connections.

Driving Action and Results: When you provide valuable insights, you inspire your audience to take action. Your insights can motivate them to implement new strategies, adopt best practices, or explore new opportunities. By sharing insights that lead to tangible outcomes, you become a catalyst for positive change and professional growth.

Positioning Yourself as a Resource: By consistently providing valuable insights, you position yourself as a reliable resource within your industry. Others will look to you for guidance, information, and expertise, creating opportunities for collaboration, partnerships, or leadership roles.

Staying Relevant and Competitive: Sharing valuable insights keeps you informed and up to date with the latest trends and developments in your industry. This allows you to stay ahead of the curve and remain relevant, ensuring you can offer valuable insights that differentiate you from competitors.

Providing valuable insights helps establish your professional reputation, build trust, foster engagement, and create meaningful connections with your audience. By consistently delivering valuable content, you become a valuable resource and an influential voice within your industry or professional community.

IMPORTANCE OF PROVIDING VALUABLE INSIGHTS TO READERS

Providing valuable insights to readers on LinkedIn is crucial for several reasons:

Establishing Credibility: Sharing valuable insights demonstrates your knowledge and expertise in your field. It positions you as a credible source of information and increases trust in your expertise.

Building Trust: When readers perceive your insights as valuable and helpful, they are more likely to trust you and your opinions. This trust can lead to stronger professional relationships, collaboration opportunities, or even potential business opportunities.

Creating Thought Leadership: Regularly providing valuable insights helps position you as a thought leader in your industry. It shows that you have a deep understanding of the subject matter and can contribute meaningful perspectives and ideas.

Engaging Your Audience: Valuable insights capture the attention of your audience and encourage them to actively engage with your content. This can lead to more comments, likes, shares, and discussions, expanding your reach and increasing your influence on the platform.

Adding Practical Value: When you provide insights that offer practical advice, solutions, or actionable steps, you provide tangible value to your readers. This helps them address challenges, learn new skills, or make informed decisions, enhancing their professional growth and success.

Fostering Relationships: Valuable insights help foster meaningful connections with your audience. When you consistently offer insights that resonate with them and provide value, you build a loyal following and create a community of individuals who appreciate and engage with your content.

Differentiating Yourself: In a crowded professional landscape, providing valuable insights sets you apart from others. It helps distinguish you as a knowledgeable professional and can make your content stand out amidst the noise.

Driving Engagement and Conversations: Valuable insights often spark discussions, debates, and conversations amongst your audience. This engagement not only strengthens your relationships but also generates additional perspectives and insights that enrich the overall conversation.

Staying Relevant: By sharing timely and valuable insights, you stay current with the latest trends, developments, and industry news. This positions you as someone who is well-informed and adapts to the evolving landscape, ensuring your content remains relevant and valuable to your audience.

By providing valuable insights, you establish credibility, build trust, engage your audience, and position yourself as a thought leader in your industry. Ultimately, it can lead to professional growth, increased visibility, and opportunities for collaboration and success.

PRESENTING DATA IN AN EASY-TO-UNDERSTAND FORMAT

Presenting data in an easy-to-understand format is crucial for effectively communicating information and insights to your audience on LinkedIn. Here are some tips for presenting data in a way that is user-friendly and accessible:

Visualize the Data: Use charts, graphs, or other visual representations to present your data. Visuals make complex information easier to comprehend and allow viewers to quickly grasp the main points or trends. Choose the appropriate type of visual representation based on the nature of your data (e.g., bar charts, pie charts, line graphs).

Keep it Simple: Simplify your data visualization by focusing on the most important aspects. Include only the necessary data points and remove any clutter or unnecessary details. Simplification makes it easier for viewers to understand and interpret the data.

Use Clear Labels and Titles: Clearly label each element of your data visualization, including axes, data points, and categories. Provide concise and descriptive titles for your visualizations that convey the main message or purpose of the data.

Provide Context: Place your data in context to make it more informative. Use captions, subtitles, or additional text to explain the significance of the data, highlight relevant trends or patterns, or provide any necessary background information. This helps viewers interpret and understand the data more effectively.

Provide Key Takeaways: Include key takeaways or summarized findings alongside your data visualization. These concise statements highlight the main insights derived from the data and provide a quick understanding of the key points you want to convey.

Use Colors and Formatting Intentionally: Use colors strategically to highlight specific data points or categories. Ensure that the color choices are easily distinguishable and do not cause confusion. Consistent and thoughtful formatting enhances the readability and visual appeal of your data visualization.

Consider Usability on Mobile Devices: As LinkedIn is accessed on various devices, including mobile, ensure your data visualization is easily viewable and interpretable on smaller screens. Optimize font sizes, adjust the layout, and use responsive design principles to ensure a smooth experience across different devices.

Provide Data Sources and Methodology: For the sake of transparency and credibility, clearly state the sources of your data and provide information on the methodology used to collect or analyze it. This adds authenticity and allows viewers to assess the reliability of the data.

Test and Iterate: Test your data visualization with a few individuals or colleagues before sharing it publicly. Gather feedback and make adjustments as needed to ensure that the data is presented clearly and effectively.

Remember, the goal is to present data in a way that allows your audience to understand and interpret the information easily. By employing these best practices for data presentation, you can effectively convey your message, support your arguments, and engage your audience on LinkedIn.

ENGAGING YOUR AUDIENCE

ENCOURAGING COMMENTS, LIKES, AND SHARES ON YOUR POSTS

Encouraging comments, likes, and shares on your LinkedIn posts can help increase engagement, expand your reach, and enhance the visibility of your content. Here are some effective strategies to encourage these interactions:

Ask Thought-Provoking Questions: Pose questions within your posts that prompt readers to share their thoughts, experiences, or opinions. Encourage discussion by inviting them to comment with their insights or perspectives related to the topic you're discussing.

Provide Shareable Content: Create content that is valuable and share-worthy. Offer actionable tips, industry insights, or exclusive information that your audience will find valuable and want to share with their connections. Make it clear why readers should share your post and how it could benefit others in their network.

Engage with Your Audience: Actively engage with your audience by responding to comments on your posts. Show appreciation for their input, answer their questions, and engage in meaningful conversations. By being responsive and engaged, you encourage further interaction and demonstrate your commitment to building a community around your content.

Call-to-Action (CTA): Include a clear and direct call-to-action at the end of your posts. Prompt your audience to like, comment, or share your post if they found it valuable or if they resonate with your message. Be explicit in what action you want them to take. For example, you can say, "Like this post if you agree" or "Share your thoughts in the comments below."

Incorporate Visual Prompts: Include visual prompts within your posts to encourage engagement. Use arrows, icons, or attention-grabbing visuals to direct the viewer's attention to the desired action, such as "Like," "Comment," or "Share."

Collaborate and Tag Others: Collaborate with other LinkedIn users or thought leaders in your industry and tag them in your posts. This can help increase visibility and encourage them to engage with your content by commenting or sharing it with their network.

Share Personal Stories or Experiences: Connect with your audience on a personal level by sharing relatable stories or experiences. This can create an emotional connection and prompt readers to engage by sharing their own stories or thoughts in the comments.

Participate in LinkedIn Groups: Engage with relevant LinkedIn groups by sharing your content and actively participating in discussions. Building connections and contributing valuable insights in these groups can lead to increased engagement with your own posts.

Consistently Provide Value: Consistently deliver valuable content that resonates with your audience. When your audience finds consistent value in your posts, they are more likely to engage, like, comment, and share them with their network.

By implementing these strategies, you can encourage your LinkedIn audience to actively engage with your content, resulting in increased visibility, broader reach, and meaningful interactions that contribute to your professional growth and success.

TECHNIQUES FOR FOSTERING MEANINGFUL CONVERSATIONS

Fostering meaningful conversations on LinkedIn is essential for building relationships, expanding your network, and creating a vibrant community around your content. Here are some techniques to help you facilitate and contribute to meaningful conversations:

Ask Open-Ended Questions: Pose open-ended questions that invite diverse opinions and perspectives. Encourage your audience to share their thoughts, experiences, or insights related to the topic you're discussing. Open-ended questions foster deeper conversation and allow for different viewpoints to be shared.

Respond Promptly and Thoughtfully: Be responsive to comments on your posts and engage in thoughtful conversations. Respond to comments in a timely manner, addressing the points raised and showing genuine interest in others' perspectives. This encourages others to continue the conversation and creates a sense of community.

Be Respectful and Constructive: Foster an environment of respect and constructive dialogue. Value the opinions and experiences of others, even if they differ from your own. Encourage discussion by asking follow-up questions, seeking clarification, and offering insights that contribute to the conversation in a positive and respectful manner.

Acknowledge and Appreciate Contributions: Show appreciation for those who contribute to the conversation. Like and reply to comments to acknowledge the contributions and insights shared by others. This recognition fosters engagement and encourages further participation.

Share Personal Experiences: Share personal anecdotes or experiences that relate to the topic at hand. Offering a personal touch can invite others to share their own stories or insights and contribute to the conversation based on their unique experiences.

Build on Others' Ideas: When engaging in conversations, build on others' ideas and expand on their points. Add value to the discussion by providing additional insights, examples, or supporting evidence. This demonstrates active listening and encourages others to continue sharing their thoughts.

Encourage Active Listening: Encourage others to actively listen and respond to each other's comments. Tag individuals or refer back to previous comments to draw attention to relevant contributions and encourage further engagement among participants.

Create a Safe and Inclusive Space: Foster a safe and inclusive environment where everyone feels comfortable contributing to the conversation. Be mindful of fostering a positive and welcoming atmosphere, free from derogatory or disrespectful language. Encourage diverse viewpoints and ensure that everyone's perspectives are respected.

Summarize and Synthesize: Summarize and synthesize the key points or themes emerging from the conversation. This helps create cohesion and encourages participants to reflect on the discussion as a whole, leading to deeper insights and meaningful exchanges.

Share Additional Resources: Offer additional resources, articles, or references that may enrich the conversation and provide further insights. Share relevant links or recommend books, research studies, or industry reports that expand on the topic being discussed. This adds value to the conversation and encourages further exploration and learning.

By utilizing these techniques, you can foster meaningful conversations on LinkedIn, engage your audience, and create a thriving community built around insightful and valuable discussions.

RESPONDING TO COMMENTS AND ENGAGING WITH YOUR AUDIENCE

Responding to comments and engaging with your audience on LinkedIn is a crucial aspect of building relationships, fostering connections, and cultivating a vibrant community around your content. Here are some tips for effectively responding to comments and engaging with your audience:

Respond Promptly: Aim to respond to comments in a timely manner. This shows that you value and appreciate the engagement of your audience. Timely responses help keep the conversation flowing and demonstrate your commitment to fostering meaningful interactions.

Show Appreciation: Express gratitude and appreciation for the comments and contributions from your audience. Let them know that you value their insights, experiences, and perspectives. A simple thank you can go a long way in building rapport and fostering a positive connection.

Be Genuine and Authentic: Engage with your audience in a sincere and authentic manner. Be yourself and let your true personality shine through in your responses. This helps build trust and connection with your audience.

Provide Thoughtful Responses: Take the time to craft thoughtful and meaningful responses to comments. Address the specific points raised, ask follow-up questions, and provide additional insights or perspectives. Show that you have read and understood their comments, and respond in a way that adds value to the conversation.

Encourage Further Discussion: Foster further engagement by asking open-ended questions or inviting others to share their thoughts or experiences related to the topic. Encourage a healthy and constructive exchange of ideas, opinions, and insights among your audience members.

Be Respectful and Constructive: Maintain a respectful and constructive tone in your responses, even if there are differing opinions or points of view. Encourage others to share their perspectives, and respond with understanding and empathy. Avoid engaging in arguments or personal attacks.

Seek Opportunities for Connection: Look for opportunities to connect with your audience on a personal level. Find common interests, experiences, or challenges that can serve as a basis for deeper conversations and stronger connections.

Be Proactive in Engagement: Don't wait for comments to come to you. Take the initiative to engage with your audience by actively seeking out and participating in discussions related to your content or industry. Comment on other posts, ask questions, and contribute valuable insights to attract engagement with your own content.

Monitor and Moderate: Keep an eye on the comments section of your posts, ensuring that conversations remain respectful and on-topic. If necessary, gently redirect discussions or address any inappropriate comments in a professional and diplomatic manner.

Continuously Engage with New Comments: Engage with new comments as they come in, even on older posts. This demonstrates your ongoing commitment to fostering engagement and keeps the conversation alive.

By effectively responding to comments and engaging with your audience, you create meaningful connections, foster a sense of community, and establish yourself as a trusted and valued member within the LinkedIn ecosystem. Your engagement efforts contribute to the overall success and impact of your content on the platform.

PROMOTING YOUR LINKEDIN POSTS

LEVERAGING LINKEDIN GROUPS AND COMMUNITIES

Leveraging LinkedIn groups and communities can be a powerful strategy for expanding your network, establishing thought leadership, and engaging with like-minded professionals. Here are some tips for effectively leveraging LinkedIn groups and communities:

Identify Relevant Groups: Find and join LinkedIn groups that align with your professional interests, industry, or areas of expertise. Look for active and engaged groups that have a significant number of members and regular discussions related to your field.

Engage in Conversations: Actively participate in group discussions by sharing insights, asking questions, and offering your expertise. Contribute valuable content and engage with others' posts and comments. This helps establish your presence within the group and positions you as a valuable member.

Share Valuable Content: Share your own content, such as articles, blog posts, videos, or resources, within relevant groups. Make sure to follow group rules and guidelines regarding self-promotion. Share content that is genuinely valuable, educational, and aligns with the interests of the group members.

Start Discussions: Initiate discussions on relevant topics to spark conversations within the group. Pose thoughtful questions, share industry news, or seek advice from other members. Encourage others to share their insights and experiences, fostering engagement and interaction.

Network and Connect: Leverage LinkedIn groups and communities to connect with like-minded professionals, industry experts, or potential clients. Engage in meaningful conversations and proactively reach out to individuals who share common interests or can offer valuable connections.

Demonstrate Thought Leadership: Actively participate in group discussions by sharing your expertise, insights, and perspectives. Provide valuable advice, industry knowledge, and best practices. Consistently offering valuable contributions helps establish yourself as a thought leader within the group.

Stay Active and Consistent: Regularly engage with LinkedIn groups by dedicating time each week to participate in discussions, share content, and interact with other members. Demonstrate your commitment and active involvement to build credibility and maintain visibility within the community.

Respect Group Guidelines and Etiquette: Familiarize yourself with the rules and guidelines of each group you join. Follow the code of conduct, respect the group's purpose, and engage in a professional and respectful manner. Be mindful of self-promotion or overly sales-oriented behavior that may not be appropriate within certain groups.

Monitor and Evaluate: Monitor the discussions and activities within LinkedIn groups to identify emerging trends, topics, or opportunities for engagement. Evaluate the impact of your participation and assess which groups provide the most value and engagement for your professional goals.

Create Your Own Group: Consider starting your own LinkedIn group around a specific interest, industry, or niche. This allows you to create a community, set the discussion agenda, and establish yourself as a community leader within your chosen subject area.

By effectively leveraging LinkedIn groups and communities, you can expand your network, stay connected with industry peers, and enhance your professional presence on the platform. Engaging in meaningful conversations, providing valuable contributions, and fostering a sense of community within relevant groups can lead to new connections, opportunities, and professional growth.

STRATEGIES FOR PROMOTING YOUR CONTENT TO INCREASE VISIBILITY

To increase the visibility of your content on LinkedIn, here are some strategies to effectively promote your posts:

Optimize Your Profile: Ensure that your LinkedIn profile is complete, professional, and optimized. Use keywords related to your industry or expertise throughout your profile to improve the chances of your content being discovered organically.

Write Compelling Headlines: Craft attention-grabbing headlines for your posts that pique curiosity and entice users to click. A compelling headline increases the likelihood of engagement and encourages users to share your content with their networks.

Network and Engage: Actively engage with your connections and relevant LinkedIn groups. Like, comment on, and share the content of others to build relationships and encourage reciprocity. By engaging with others, you increase the visibility of your own profile and content.

Share at Optimal Times: Share your content when your audience is most likely to be active on LinkedIn. Typically, mornings on weekdays are considered prime times for engagement. Experiment with different posting times, track engagement metrics, and adjust your strategy accordingly.

Leverage Hashtags: Include relevant hashtags in your posts to increase discoverability. Research popular and industry-specific hashtags to reach a broader audience and amplify the visibility of your content.

Cross-Promote on Other Channels: Promote your LinkedIn content across other social media channels, such as Twitter, Facebook, or Instagram. Share snippets or teasers of your LinkedIn posts with links back to the full content on LinkedIn. This drives traffic and expands the reach of your content beyond the LinkedIn platform.

Encourage Employee Advocacy: Enlist the support of your colleagues or employees to amplify the reach of your content. Encourage them to like, comment on, and share your content within their networks. This increases the visibility of your posts to their connections and potentially expands your reach.

Utilize LinkedIn Sponsored Content: Consider using LinkedIn's sponsored content feature to boost the visibility of your posts to a wider audience. This paid advertising option allows you to target specific demographics, industries, or interests to reach potential new connections and amplify the reach of your content.

Collaborate with Influencers: Collaborate with influencers or thought leaders in your industry by featuring them in your content or seeking their input. When they engage with or share your content, it can significantly increase its reach and visibility.

Analyze and Optimize: Regularly review the performance and engagement metrics of your posts using LinkedIn's analytics tools. Analyze the data to identify patterns, themes, or content types that resonate best with your audience. Use this information to optimize your future content strategy and increase visibility.

By implementing these strategies, you can effectively promote your content on LinkedIn, increase its visibility, reach a wider audience, and drive engagement with your posts. Remember to regularly assess your efforts, evaluate the impact of your promotion strategies, and adapt your approach based on the insights gained.

CROSS-PROMOTING ACROSS OTHER SOCIAL MEDIA PLATFORMS

Cross-promoting your LinkedIn content across other social media platforms can help increase its visibility, reach new audiences, and drive engagement. Here are some strategies for effectively cross-promoting your LinkedIn content:

Tease and Link: Create short teasers or snippets of your LinkedIn posts and share them on platforms like Twitter, Facebook, Instagram, or YouTube. Include a catchy headline or an intriguing question to pique curiosity, and provide a link to the full post on LinkedIn. This encourages followers on other platforms to click through and engage with your LinkedIn content.

Repurpose Content: Adapt your LinkedIn posts into different formats suitable for other social media platforms. For example, you can turn a text-based post into an image quote, create a short video summarizing key points, or create an infographic showcasing the main insights. Tailor the content to the specific requirements and norms of each platform.

Leverage Visual Content: Visual content tends to perform well on social media platforms. Share visually appealing images, infographics, or videos from your LinkedIn posts on other platforms. Use relevant and attention-grabbing visuals to capture the interest of your audience and entice them to explore your LinkedIn content.

Utilize LinkedIn Sharing Buttons: Take advantage of LinkedIn's sharing buttons on your blog or website. Whenever you publish a new blog post or article, include LinkedIn sharing buttons to allow readers to easily share your content on their LinkedIn profiles. This helps widen the reach of your content within professional networks.

Engage with LinkedIn Communities: Engage in industry-specific or interest-based LinkedIn communities and groups. Actively participate in discussions, offer insights, and share relevant content from your LinkedIn posts. This allows you to cross-promote your content while adding value to the community and sparking interest in your LinkedIn profile.

Collaborate with Influencers or Partners: Collaborate with influencers or complementary professionals in your industry. Create joint content, such as interviews, articles, or discussions, and share it across both your LinkedIn profiles and respective social media platforms. This expands your reach by tapping into their audience while providing unique value to your own followers.

Use Social Media Management Tools: Utilize social media management tools to schedule and automate cross-promotion of your LinkedIn content. By pre-scheduling posts across multiple platforms, you can ensure consistent visibility and engagement while saving time and effort.

Track and Analyze Engagement: Monitor the engagement metrics of your cross-promotion efforts. Analyze which platforms perform best, which types of content resonate with your audience, and adapt your strategy accordingly. Use the insights gained to continually refine your cross-promotion approach.

Remember, while cross-promoting on other social media platforms is valuable, always ensure that your content is tailored to each platform's unique audience and usage patterns. By effectively cross-promoting your LinkedIn content, you can increase its reach, drive engagement, and establish a cohesive and impactful online presence.

ANALYZING AND OPTIMIZING LINKEDIN METRICS

UNDERSTANDING LINKEDIN'S ANALYTICS TOOLS

LinkedIn offers several analytics tools to help you track the performance and engagement of your content. Here is an overview of LinkedIn's analytics tools:

LinkedIn Page Analytics: If you have a LinkedIn Company Page, you can access LinkedIn Page Analytics. This tool provides insights into the overall performance of your page, including follower demographics, engagement metrics, and post reach. It helps you understand which content resonates with your audience and provides data to refine your content strategy.

Content Analytics: Content Analytics provides detailed metrics for your individual LinkedIn posts. It includes data on impressions, clicks, engagement rate, shares, and more. You can assess the effectiveness of your content and identify trends or patterns that can guide future content creation.

Visitor Analytics: Visitor Analytics provides information about the visitors to your LinkedIn profile, including their demographics, industry, and location. It helps you understand who is viewing your profile, which can inform your networking and engagement strategies.

Followers Analytics: Followers Analytics provides insights into the demographics, growth rate, and engagement behavior of your LinkedIn followers. It allows you to understand your audience's characteristics and preferences, helping you tailor your content and engagement strategies to better serve them.

LinkedIn Campaign Manager: LinkedIn Campaign Manager is a comprehensive ad management tool that provides detailed analytics for your LinkedIn advertising campaigns. You can track metrics such as impressions, clicks, conversions, and more, enabling you to optimize and measure the effectiveness of your campaigns.

LinkedIn Sales Navigator: LinkedIn Sales Navigator offers analytics and insights focused on sales and lead generation. It provides information about profile views, lead recommendations, and engagement with your network. This tool is particularly useful for sales professionals and teams looking to track their sales activities and identify potential leads.

By utilizing these LinkedIn analytics tools, you can gain valuable insights into the performance of your content, audience engagement, and follower demographics. This data allows you to make data-driven decisions, refine your strategy, and maximize your impact on the platform. Regularly analyzing and assessing these analytics will help you optimize your LinkedIn presence for better visibility and engagement.

INTERPRETING KEY METRICS TO ASSESS POST PERFORMANCE

Interpreting key metrics is essential for assessing the performance of your LinkedIn posts. By analyzing these metrics, you can determine the effectiveness of your post and make necessary adjustments to optimize future content. Some key metrics to consider when interpreting post performance include:

Impressions: Impressions represent the number of times your post was displayed on LinkedIn. Higher impression numbers indicate that your post is reaching a larger audience.

Click-through Rate (CTR): CTR measures the percentage of impressions that resulted in a click. A high CTR indicates that your post is engaging and compelling enough to prompt viewers to take action.

Likes, Comments, and Shares: These engagement metrics show how well your post resonates with your audience. Likes indicate approval or agreement, comments signify conversations and discussions sparked by your post, and shares demonstrate that your content is valuable and worth sharing with others.

Follower Growth: Monitoring the number of new followers gained after a post can indicate the effectiveness of your content in attracting and retaining an audience.

Conversion Metrics: If your post includes a call-to-action, such as visiting a website or downloading a resource, tracking conversion metrics can help you determine the success of your post in driving desired actions.

Engagement Rate: This metric calculates the overall engagement of your post by considering the number of engagements (likes, comments, shares) relative to the number of impressions. A higher engagement rate suggests that your post is resonating well with your audience.

When interpreting these metrics, it's important to compare them against your goals and benchmarks. Look for trends and patterns to identify what content performs best and where improvements can be made. Consider experimenting with different types of content, headlines, visuals, or posting times to see how they impact your metrics. Regularly reviewing and analyzing metrics will help you refine your LinkedIn posting strategy and maximize your success on the platform.

USING DATA TO OPTIMIZE FUTURE LINKEDIN POSTS

Using data to optimize future LinkedIn posts is crucial for continually improving your content strategy and maximizing engagement. Here are some key steps to effectively utilize data:

Analyze Post Performance: Review the metrics mentioned earlier to identify patterns and trends in post performance. Look for posts that garnered high engagement, click-through rates, or conversions, and determine the factors that contributed to their success.

Identify Successful Content Themes: Analyze the content of your top-performing posts. Identify common themes, topics, or formats that consistently resonate with your audience. This will help you understand the preferences and interests of your LinkedIn followers.

Refine Your Target Audience: Use data to understand the demographics and behavior of your LinkedIn audience. This information can be found in LinkedIn analytics or through third-party tools. By knowing the characteristics of your audience, you can tailor your content to their needs and preferences.

Experiment with Different Formats and Presentation Styles: Based on your analysis, consider trying different formats like videos, infographics, or long-form posts. Experiment with various presentation styles, such as storytelling, providing tips and insights, or sharing personal experiences, to see what resonates best with your audience.

Optimize Headlines and Descriptions: Analyze the headlines and descriptions of your high-performing posts and identify patterns in their effectiveness. Use this knowledge to craft compelling and attention-grabbing headlines for future posts. Consider incorporating keywords relevant to your target audience for better discoverability.

Test Posting Times: Experiment with different days and times to publish your posts. Observe when your audience is most active on LinkedIn and schedule your posts accordingly. Analyzing data on engagement rates during various time periods can help you determine the best posting times for maximum visibility and reach.

Engage with Your Audience: Actively monitor and respond to comments, questions, and messages on your LinkedIn posts. Engaging with your audience not only strengthens existing relationships but also provides insights into their preferences and needs, helping you optimize future content.

Measure and Adjust: Continuously evaluate the performance of your LinkedIn posts by analyzing the relevant metrics. Refine your content strategy based on the data and feedback received, making adjustments to improve engagement and reach.

Remember, data analysis and optimization are ongoing processes. Regularly track results, stay updated with LinkedIn updates and algorithm changes, and adapt your strategy accordingly to stay ahead of the curve and achieve better results with your LinkedIn posts.

POST EXAMPLES AND TEMPLATES

COLLECTION OF SUCCESSFUL LINKEDIN POSTS AND THEIR ANALYSIS

Here are 20 more examples of successful LinkedIn posts and their analysis:

Post 1: Headline: "5 Key Strategies for Effective Project Management" Content: The post provided insights and practical advice on project management strategies. It included actionable steps, real-life examples, and tips for successful project execution. The clear structure and concise writing style made the post easily digestible and engaging.

Success Factors:

Actionable Advice: The post offered specific strategies that project managers could apply in their work, making it valuable and actionable for the target audience.

Real-Life Examples: Including real examples helped illustrate the strategies and made the post relatable and applicable.

Clear Structure: A clear and organized structure made the post easy to read and follow.

Post 2: Headline: "The Future of Remote Work: How to Thrive in a Virtual Work Environment" Content: The post discussed the benefits and challenges of remote work and provided tips for success in a virtual work environment. It addressed the increasing trend of remote work and offered practical insights for individuals and organizations adapting to this new way of work.

Success Factors:

Timeliness: Addressing the growing interest in remote work made the post relevant and timely.

Actionable Tips: Providing practical advice and strategies for thriving in a virtual work environment added value to the post.

Future Focus: Exploring the future of remote work and offering insights on adapting to this shift captured the attention of the target audience.

Post 3: Headline: "Building a Personal Brand: Why it Matters and How to Do It Right" Content: The post discussed the importance of personal branding for professional success and provided guidance on building a strong personal brand. It included tips on creating a personal brand statement, utilizing social media, and showcasing expertise.

Success Factors:

Importance of Personal Branding: Addressing a key topic of interest for professionals looking to enhance their personal brand resonated with the target audience.

Practical Tips: Offering actionable advice and steps

to build a personal brand provided clear guidance for readers.

Expertise Positioning: Highlighting the author's own experience and success in personal branding added credibility and authority to the post.

Post 4: Headline: "The Power of Networking: How to Build Meaningful Connections in a Digital World" Content: The post discussed the importance of networking for personal and professional growth and shared strategies for building meaningful connections online. It emphasized the value of authentic relationships and provided tips for effectively networking on LinkedIn.

Success Factors:

Relevance: Networking is a key interest for professionals, and addressing it in the context of a digital world made the post highly relevant.

Authenticity: Emphasizing the importance of authentic connections and providing tips on building genuine relationships resonated with the target audience.

Specific Tips for LinkedIn: Providing strategies specific to networking on LinkedIn showcased the author's expertise and offered actionable insights for the platform's users.

Post 5: Headline: "The Art of Negotiation: Key

Techniques for Successful Deals" Content: The post shared expert tips and techniques for negotiating effectively, covering topics like preparation, active listening, and finding win-win solutions. It provided actionable advice for professionals across various industries and roles.

Success Factors:

Expert Advice: Offering insights and techniques from negotiation experts added credibility and value to the post.

Actionable Tips: Providing practical steps and techniques that readers could apply in their own negotiations made the post valuable to the target audience.

Broad Applicability: Addressing negotiation skills that are relevant across industries and roles widened the potential audience and increased engagement.

Post 6: Headline: "The Power of Emotional Intelligence in Leadership: Why EQ Matters" Content: The post highlighted the significance of emotional intelligence (EQ) in leadership and provided insights into its impact on team dynamics and overall success. It discussed the key components of EQ and offered tips for developing and enhancing emotional intelligence.

Success Factors:

Leadership Focus: Addressing the importance of emotional intelligence specifically in leadership appealed to professionals in managerial and leadership roles.

Educational Value: Offering insights into EQ and practical suggestions for developing emotional intelligence added educational value to the post.

Relevance: Emotional intelligence is a significant topic in workplace environments, making the post highly relevant to the target audience.

Post 7: Headline: "Navigating Career Transitions: Strategies for Successful Switches" Content: The post provided guidance and tips for professionals navigating career transitions, including changing industries or roles. It addressed common challenges and provided actionable steps and resources to support individuals in their career switches.

Success Factors:

Valuable Resources: Sharing resources such as career transition frameworks, job search platforms, or networking groups added value to the post.

Actionable Steps: Offering practical strategies and specific steps for career transitions made the post engaging and useful.

Empathy: Acknowledging the challenges involved in

career transitions and providing support and reassurance resonated with the target audience.

Post 8: Headline: "The Impact of Artificial Intelligence on the Future of Work" Content: The post explored the influence of artificial intelligence (AI) on the future of work and discussed potential opportunities and challenges. It offered insights into how professionals can adapt to and thrive in an AI-driven workplace.

Success Factors:

Timeliness: Addressing the growing interest and concerns regarding AI in the workplace made the post highly relevant.

Future Focus: Exploring the potential impact of AI on work and offering insights into adaptation strategies captured the attention of the target audience.

Balance: Presenting both opportunities and challenges of AI in the workplace showcased a balanced and comprehensive view, adding credibility to the post.

Post 9: Headline: "Effective Time Management Strategies for Busy Professionals" Content: The post shared practical time management strategies aimed at busy professionals and offered tips for prioritization, delegation, and productivity improvement. It addressed the common challenge of managing time effectively in demanding work environments.

Success Factors:

Relevance: Time management is a universal concern for professionals, making the post highly relevant to a wide audience.

Practical Tips: Providing actionable strategies for improving time management and productivity added value to the post.

Concise and Digestible: Presenting the tips in a concise and easily digestible format made the post engaging and accessible.

Post 10: Headline: "Tips for Creating a Standout Resume: Get Noticed in the Job Market" Content: The post shared expert tips and advice for crafting a standout resume, focusing on strategies for highlighting achievements, optimizing formatting, and tailoring the content for specific job applications. It aimed to help professionals stand out in a competitive job market.

Success Factors:

Expert Advice: Sharing insights and techniques from resume writing experts added credibility and value to the post.

Actionable Tips: Offering specific recommendations and steps for improving resumes made the post practical and applicable for job seekers.

Relevance: Resumes are a critical component of job applications, making the post highly relevant to professionals seeking employment opportunities.

Post 11: Headline: "Building a Diverse and Inclusive Workplace: Strategies for Success" Content: The post discussed the importance of diversity and inclusion in the workplace, highlighting the benefits and sharing strategies for achieving a more inclusive environment. It offered practical suggestions for promoting diversity, fostering inclusion, and addressing bias.

Success Factors:

Timeliness: Addressing the increasing emphasis on diversity and inclusion in workplaces made the topic highly relevant and compelling.

Practical Strategies: Offering actionable steps and strategies for creating a more diverse and inclusive workplace provided clear guidance for the target audience.

Education and Awareness: Providing insights into the benefits of diversity and inclusion and raising awareness of bias contributed to the post's effectiveness.

Post 12: Headline: "The Importance of Mental Health in the Workplace: Strategies for Support" Content: The post explored the significance of mental health in the workplace and provided strategies for supporting employee well-being. It addressed key areas such as reducing stigma, creating supportive environments, and offering resources for mental health support.

Success Factors:

Social Impact: Addressing mental health and promoting workplace well-being contributed to the post's overall engagement and resonance.

Practical Support: Offering concrete strategies and resources for supporting mental health in the workplace added value to the post.

Sensitivity and Empathy: Demonstrating sensitivity and empathy towards mental health challenges created a safe and supportive space for discussions.

Post 13: Headline: "Women Empowerment in Business: Breaking Barriers and Shattering Glass Ceilings" Content: The post highlighted the challenges women face in the business world and discussed strategies for empowering women and promoting gender equality. It celebrated successful stories of women in business and offered guidance for overcoming obstacles.

Success Factors:

Social Impact: Addressing gender equality and the empowerment of women resonated with a broad audience passionate about diversity and inclusion.

Inspirational Stories: Sharing success stories of women in business inspired and motivated the target audience.

Actionable Strategies: Providing actionable steps and advice for empowering women and overcoming barriers made the post practical and valuable.

Post 14: Headline: "Navigating the Job Interview Process: Tips for Success" Content: The post offered tips and guidance for effectively navigating the job interview process, covering areas like interview preparation, answering common interview questions, and post-interview follow-up. It aimed to support individuals in achieving success in their job search.

Success Factors:

Practical Guidance: Offering practical advice and suggestions for job interviews provided clear direction for job seekers.

Expert Tips: Sharing insights and best practices from interview experts added credibility and value to the post.

Relevance: Job interviews are a crucial aspect of the job search process, making the post highly relevant to professionals seeking employment.

Post 15: Headline: "Effective Communication Skills for Leadership Success" Content: The post discussed the importance of effective communication skills in leadership and provided strategies for enhancing communication abilities. It covered areas such as active listening, nonverbal communication, and clear messaging.

Success Factors:

Leadership Focus: Addressing communication skills specifically in the context of leadership appealed to professionals in managerial and leadership roles.

Actionable Strategies: Offering actionable steps and techniques for improving communication skills made the post valuable for the target audience.

Relevance: Communication skills are essential in various professional settings, making the post relevant to a broad audience.

Post 16: Headline: "The Power of Personal Development: Invest in Yourself for Success" Content: The post emphasized the importance of personal development for professional growth and success. It discussed various areas of personal development, such as continuous learning, goal setting, and self-reflection, and offered actionable strategies for self-improvement.

Success Factors:

Inspiring and Motivating: Highlighting the benefits of personal development and providing strategies to support individual growth motivated the target audience.

Actionable Tips: Offering practical steps and techniques for personal development made the post valuable and applicable for readers.

Empowerment: Encouraging individuals to invest in themselves and take ownership of their personal growth added an empowering element to the post.

Post 17: Headline: "Mastering Work-Life Balance: Strategies for Thriving in a Busy World" Content: The post explored the challenges of achieving work-life balance and shared strategies for finding equilibrium and prioritizing well-being. It offered practical tips for managing time, setting boundaries, and incorporating self-care.

Success Factors:

Relevance: Work-life balance is a common concern, making the post highly relatable and engaging for the target audience.

Practical Advice: Providing actionable strategies and tips for achieving work-life balance made the post valuable and useful.

Empathy: Acknowledging the challenges individuals face and offering support and guidance resonated with readers.

Post 18: Headline: "Navigating Career Growth: Strategies for Advancement and Promotion" Content: The post discussed strategies for career growth and offered insights into advancing within one's profession. It covered areas like skill development, networking, and mentorship, aiming to support professionals in achieving their career goals.

Success Factors:

Professional Growth Focus: Addressing career advancement resonated with professionals seeking to progress in their careers.

Practical Strategies: Offering actionable steps and suggestions for career growth and promotion added value and clarity to the post.

Empowerment: Encouraging individuals to take control of their career growth through skill development and networking added an empowering element to the post.

Post 19: Headline: "Building Resilience in the Workplace: Overcoming Challenges and Bouncing Back" Content: The post discussed the importance of resilience in the workplace and provided strategies for developing and strengthening resilience. It addressed coping with adversity, managing stress, and bouncing back from setbacks.

Success Factors:

Relevance: Resilience is a valuable skill in professional settings, making the post highly relevant to the target audience.

Practical Advice: Offering practical strategies and techniques for building resilience in the workplace provided clear guidance and added value to the post.

Empathy: Acknowledging the challenges professionals face and providing support and guidance resonated with readers seeking resilience.

Post 20: Headline: "Creating a Positive Work Culture: Strategies for Fostering Engagement and Happiness" Content: The post explored the importance of a positive work culture and shared strategies for fostering employee engagement and happiness. It discussed areas such as leadership, team collaboration, and recognition, aiming to support organizations in creating a positive work environment.

Success Factors:

Company Culture Focus: Addressing work culture resonated with professionals seeking to improve their organizations' environments.

Actionable Strategies: Offering practical steps and

approaches for fostering engagement and happiness at work made the post valuable for leaders and managers.

Relevance: A positive work culture is essential for employee satisfaction and organizational success, making the post highly relevant and appealing.

POST TEMPLATES FOR DIFFERENT CONTENT

Here are post templates for different types of content:

Template 1: Tips Headline: [Insert concise and attention-grabbing headline]

Introduction: In today's post, I wanted to share some valuable tips on [topic]. Whether you're [target audience], these tips can help you [desired outcome].

Tip 1: [Insert Tip] Description: [Explain the tip and its benefits]

Tip 2: [Insert Tip] Description: [Explain the tip and its benefits]

Tip 3: [Insert Tip] Description: [Explain the tip and its benefits]

Conclusion: I hope you find these tips useful in [achieving the desired outcome]. If you have any questions or additional tips to share, feel free to comment below!

Template 2: Industry Insights Headline: [Insert intriguing and relevant headline]

Introduction: In today's post, I wanted to share some intriguing insights and trends within the [industry/field].

Understanding these insights can help professionals stay ahead and succeed in this dynamic landscape.

Insight 1: [Insert Insight] Description: [Explain the insight and its implications]

Insight 2: [Insert Insight] Description: [Explain the insight and its implications]

Insight 3: [Insert Insight] Description: [Explain the insight and its implications]

Conclusion: These industry insights shed light on the current and future direction of the [industry/field]. How do you see these trends impacting our work? Share your thoughts in the comments!

Template 3: Personal Stories Headline: [Insert captivating and relatable headline]

Introduction: In today's post, I wanted to take a moment to share a personal story that I believe many of you can relate to. It's a story of [experience/emotion/achievement] that has shaped my [industry/field] journey.

Story: [Share your personal story, including the challenges faced, lessons learned, and the impact it had on your professional growth]

Key Takeaway: [Summarize the key lesson or insight gained from the personal story]

Conclusion: I hope that by sharing this personal story, it resonates with some of you and inspires you on your own journey. Feel free to share your own stories or reflections in the comments!

Feel free to customize these templates to suit your specific content and audience. Remember to keep your posts concise, engaging, and relevant to provide value to your LinkedIn connections.

BONUS TEMPLATES

Template 1: Ask a Question Headline: [Pose a thought-provoking question]

Introduction: I'd love to hear your thoughts on [topic]. Comment below and let's start a conversation!

Template 2: Industry Trends Headline: [Highlight an emerging trend in the industry]

Introduction: In today's rapidly evolving industry, it's crucial to stay on top of the latest trends. Here's an exciting trend that is reshaping the [industry/field].

Template 3: Celebrating Milestones Headline: [Celebrate a milestone or accomplishment]

Introduction: Today, I'm thrilled to share a personal milestone/accomplishment: [Explain the milestone/ accomplishment and its significance]. Thank you all for your support along the way!

Template 4: Book Recommendation Headline: [Recommend a valuable book for professionals]

Introduction: If you're looking to expand your knowledge in [industry/field], I highly recommend [book title]. Here's why it should be on your reading list.

Template 5: Inspirational Quote Headline: [Share a motivational quote]

Introduction: Sometimes, a few words of inspiration can make a big difference. Here's a quote that has been motivating me lately. What does it mean to you?

Template 6: Industry News Update Headline: [Highlight a recent news development in the industry]

Introduction: Stay informed on the latest news in our industry. Here's an update on [industry news topic] and its potential impact on professionals like us.

Template 7: Success Story/Case Study Headline: [Present a success story or case study]

Introduction: Today, I want to share an inspiring success story/case study that showcases the power of [industry/field]. Learn how [individual/organization] achieved remarkable results.

Template 8: Thought-Provoking Statistic Headline: [Share a surprising or thought-provoking statistic]

Introduction: Did you know that [statistic]? It's a remarkable insight that highlights the importance of [industry/field]. Here's why it matters.

Template 9: Industry Challenges and Solutions Headline: [Identify a common challenge in the industry and offer a solution]

Introduction: Many professionals in our industry face the challenge of [industry challenge]. Here's a solution that can help overcome it.

Template 10: Emerging Technologies Headline: [Discuss an emerging technology impacting the industry]

Introduction: Technology is revolutionizing our industry, and one emerging technology that has caught my attention is [technology]. Discover how it is transforming [industry/field].

Template 11: The Power of Networking Headline: [Highlight the value of networking]

Introduction: Networking plays a crucial role in professional success. Here are some tips to maximize the power of your professional network.

Template 12: Lessons Learned from Failure Headline: [Share lessons learned from a personal or industry failure]

Introduction: Failure is an inevitable part of success. Here are some valuable lessons I learned from a recent failure and how they have shaped my approach.

Template 13: Behind-the-Scenes Insights Headline: [Offer a behind-the-scenes look into your work or industry]

129

Introduction: Get an exclusive behind-the-scenes glimpse into [industry/field] and discover the inner workings of [company/project]. Join me on this journey!

Template 14: Product or Service Highlight Headline: [Promote a product or service and its benefits]

Introduction: Introducing [product/service], a game-changer in [industry/field]. Learn how it can transform your [specific benefit] and help you achieve [desired outcome].

Template 15: Quotes from Industry Influencers Headline: [Share impactful quotes from industry influencers]

Introduction: Industry influencers have a wealth of knowledge and insights. Here are some thought-provoking quotes from the most influential voices in our field.

Template 16: Share a Helpful Resource Headline: [Recommend a valuable resource for professionals]

Introduction: If you're looking for a helpful resource, look no further. Here's a resource that can help you [benefit] and enhance your professional journey.

Template 17: Highlight a Research Study Headline: [Present key findings of a relevant research study]

Introduction: Research plays a vital role in our industry. Explore the powerful insights discovered in a recent study on [research topic] and their implications for professionals.

Template 18: Predictions for the Future Headline: [Share your predictions for the future of the industry]

Introduction: As the industry evolves, it's important to envision what lies ahead. Here are my predictions for the future of [industry/field]. What do you think?

Template 19: Daily/Weekly Challenge Headline: [Present a challenge or task for professionals]

Introduction: Are you up for a challenge? Join me in this daily/weekly challenge focused on [specific skill/development area]. Let's grow together!

Template 20: Inspirational Story of Resilience Headline: [Share an inspiring story of resilience]

Introduction: Resilience is a powerful quality that can help us overcome challenges. Let me share a story of incredible resilience that has inspired me.

Feel free to modify and personalize these templates to fit your specific content and audience. Remember to keep your posts engaging, informative, and relevant to provide value to your LinkedIn connections.

CONCLUSION

Recap of key takeaways from the book

Key Takeaways from the Book "Mastering LinkedIn: A Guide to Writing Engaging Posts":

LinkedIn is a powerful professional networking platform that can bring personal and professional success if utilized effectively.

Writing engaging LinkedIn posts is essential to maximize your impact and reach a larger audience.

Understand LinkedIn's audience demographics and user behavior to tailor your content effectively.

Craft attention-grabbing headlines that attract viewers and compel them to click on your post.

Structure your LinkedIn posts in an organized and readable format, using the inverted pyramid structure and breaking down content into sections.

Harness the power of storytelling techniques to captivate your audience and convey your message effectively.

Incorporate visuals and multimedia, such as images, infographics, and videos, to enhance the visual appeal of your posts.

Add value to your posts by including data, statistics, and research to support your points and provide valuable insights to readers.

Engage your audience through meaningful conversations, encouraging comments, likes, and shares on your posts.

Promote your LinkedIn posts effectively by leveraging LinkedIn groups and communities and cross-promoting on other social media platforms.

Analyze LinkedIn metrics to understand the performance of your posts and optimize future content accordingly.

Use post examples and templates provided in the book to guide your content creation and make it more effective.

In conclusion, mastering LinkedIn involves understanding the platform's audience, crafting engaging content, utilizing storytelling techniques, leveraging visuals and data, engaging with your audience, and analyzing metrics for continuous improvement. By implementing the strategies and tips outlined in this book, you can unlock the power of LinkedIn for personal and professional success.

ENCOURAGEMENT TO APPLY THE KNOWLEDGE GAINED AND SUCCEED ON LINKEDIN

In closing, I encourage you to apply the knowledge and strategies gained from this book to succeed on LinkedIn. LinkedIn offers immense opportunities for personal and professional growth, and by implementing the techniques outlined in this guide, you can maximize your impact on the platform.

Engage with your target audience by crafting compelling and engaging posts that resonate with them. Leverage the power of storytelling, incorporate visuals and multimedia, and provide valuable insights through data and research. Foster meaningful conversations with your audience, respond to comments, and create a vibrant and engaged community.

Don't forget to promote your LinkedIn posts, leveraging LinkedIn groups, communities, and cross-promoting on other social media platforms. Analyze the performance metrics provided by LinkedIn to understand what works best and optimize future content accordingly.

Remember, LinkedIn is a dynamic and ever-evolving platform, so continuous learning and adaptation are key. Stay up to date with the latest trends and changes, experiment with different strategies, and refine your approach based on audience feedback and data.

Now, it's time to unlock the power of LinkedIn and unleash your personal and professional potential. Apply the knowledge gained from this guide, explore new possibilities, and make meaningful connections that can propel your career forward. Harness the full potential of LinkedIn and achieve the success you aspire to. Best of luck on your LinkedIn journey!

APPENDICES:

APPENDIX A: GLOSSARY OF LINKEDIN TERMS

Here is a glossary of common LinkedIn terms:

Profile: A personal page on LinkedIn that showcases your professional experience, skills, and qualifications.

Connection: Someone you are connected with on LinkedIn. Connections can consist of colleagues, classmates, mentors, or other professionals in your industry.

Endorsement: A feature that allows LinkedIn users to validate and recognize the skills and expertise of their connections.

Recommendation: A written statement by a connection endorsing your skills, experience, or work. Recommendations provide social proof and credibility to your profile.

Feed: The content stream on the LinkedIn homepage where you can see updates, posts, and articles from your connections and professional networks.

Engagement: The actions that users take on your posts, such as likes, comments, and shares. Engagement is a measure of how well your content resonates with your audience.

InMail: A messaging feature on LinkedIn that allows users to send private messages to other LinkedIn members they are not connected with.

Groups: Communities on LinkedIn where professionals with similar interests or affiliations can join to engage in discussions, share insights, and network.

Hashtags: Keywords or phrases preceded by the '#' symbol that are used to categorize and index posts on LinkedIn. Hashtags help users discover and follow specific topics or conversations.

SSI (Social Selling Index): A metric provided by LinkedIn that measures an individual's effectiveness in using LinkedIn for social selling—the process of using social platforms to identify, engage, and nurture potential buyers.

LinkedIn Pulse: A platform within LinkedIn where professionals can publish and share long-form content such as articles and blog posts.

LinkedIn Premium: A paid LinkedIn subscription service that offers features such as expanded search capabilities, access to premium insights and data, and additional messaging privileges.

Connection Request: A request sent to another LinkedIn member to connect and establish a professional relationship.

Alumni: LinkedIn users who have listed the same educational institution on their profiles. Alumni can connect and engage with each other through LinkedIn.

Showcase Page: A separate page within a company profile on LinkedIn that focuses on a specific brand, initiative, or product.

Thought Leadership: Building a reputation as an expert or authority in a particular field through sharing valuable insights, expertise, and industry knowledge on LinkedIn.

LinkedIn Learning: An online learning platform that offers a wide range of courses and tutorials on various professional skills, software, and business topics.

Company Page: A page on LinkedIn that represents a company or organization. It provides information about the company, its updates, job openings, and more.

LinkedIn Sales Navigator: A sales and prospecting tool provided by LinkedIn that helps sales professionals find and connect with potential leads and customers.

LinkedIn Analytics: Insights and data provided by LinkedIn that allow you to measure the performance of your posts, profile, and engagement metrics.

This glossary serves as a reference to help you navigate and understand the terminology commonly used on LinkedIn.

APPENDIX B: RECOMMENDED LINKEDIN RESOURCES AND TOOLS

Here are some recommended LinkedIn resources and tools to enhance your LinkedIn experience:

LinkedIn Learning: An online learning platform that provides a wide range of courses and tutorials on various professional skills, software, and business topics. LinkedIn Learning offers valuable resources for personal and professional development.

LinkedIn Help Center: The LinkedIn Help Center is a comprehensive resource that provides answers to frequently asked questions about using LinkedIn. It offers guidance on various features, settings, and troubleshooting tips.

LinkedIn Blog: The LinkedIn Blog covers a variety of topics, including platform updates, industry trends, career advice, and success stories. It is a valuable resource for staying informed about the latest LinkedIn news and best practices.

LinkedIn Sales Solutions: LinkedIn offers sales tools and solutions specifically designed for sales professionals. LinkedIn Sales Navigator, for example, provides features to help identify and engage with potential leads and customers effectively.

LinkedIn Marketing Solutions: LinkedIn's marketing solutions provide powerful advertising and marketing tools for businesses to reach their target audience on the platform. You can explore options like Sponsored Content, Sponsored InMail, and Dynamic Ads to promote your brand and engage with professionals.

LinkedIn Events: LinkedIn Events is a feature that allows you to create and promote professional events directly on the platform. It provides a seamless way to manage event details, invite attendees, and facilitate networking opportunities.

LinkedIn SlideShare: LinkedIn SlideShare is a platform where users can upload and share presentations, infographics, and documents. It is a valuable resource for accessing industry-specific presentations, research reports, and educational content.

LinkedIn Pulse: LinkedIn Pulse is a platform within LinkedIn where professionals can publish and share long-form content such as articles and blog posts. It provides an opportunity to showcase thought leadership and engage with a wider audience.

LinkedIn Alumni: LinkedIn Alumni is a feature that allows you to explore and connect with fellow alumni from your educational institutions. It can be a valuable networking tool for building connections within your alma mater's professional community.

LinkedIn Company Pages: LinkedIn Company Pages provide a space for companies to showcase their brand, share updates, and engage with their audience. Utilize this feature to follow and connect with companies relevant to your professional interests.

These resources and tools can enhance your LinkedIn experience by providing valuable learning opportunities, insights, and tools to expand your professional network and achieve your goals on the platform. Consult these resources as needed to make the most out of your LinkedIn presence.

APPENDIX C: ADDITIONAL READING AND REFERENCES

Here are some additional reading recommendations and references to further enhance your understanding of LinkedIn and maximize your success on the platform:

"LinkedIn Unlocked: Unlocking the Mystery of LinkedIn to Drive Massive Sales Through Social Selling" by Melonie Dodaro This book offers practical guidance on leveraging LinkedIn for social selling, providing strategies to generate leads and drive sales through effective networking and content creation.

"The LinkedIn Code: Unlock the Largest Online Business Social Network to Get Leads, Prospects & Clients for B2B, Professional Services and Sales & Marketing Pros" by Melonie Dodaro In this book, Dodaro provides strategies tailored to B2B professionals to effectively utilize LinkedIn for attracting leads, prospects, and clients.

"LinkedIn For Dummies" by Joel Elad Geared towards beginners, this book provides comprehensive guidance on setting up and optimizing your LinkedIn profile, connecting with others, and leveraging key features for professional success.

"Make LinkedIn Work For You: A Practical Handbook for Harnessing the Power of LinkedIn for Your Business" by Eric Butow and Kathleen Taylor This handbook covers the essentials of LinkedIn for businesses, guiding readers through profile optimization, content sharing, networking strategies, and lead generation techniques.

LinkedIn Official Blog Stay updated by regularly exploring the official LinkedIn Blog (blog.linkedin.com), which features articles and insights on platform updates, best practices, industry trends, and success stories.

"LinkedIn Marketing: An Hour a Day" by Viveka von Rosen This book provides a step-by-step guide for creating and implementing a comprehensive LinkedIn marketing strategy, including tips for content creation, engagement, and lead generation.

"The LinkedIn Playbook: Contacts to Customers. Engage. Connect. Convert." by Adam Houlahan Houlahan offers a playbook-style guide to help businesses and professionals utilize LinkedIn effectively to connect with potential customers, build relationships, and drive conversion.

LinkedIn Help Center (linkedin.com/help) The official LinkedIn Help Center is a valuable resource for finding answers to commonly asked questions and troubleshooting issues related to using LinkedIn effectively.

"LinkedIn Riches: How to Leverage LinkedIn for Business Growth and Lead Generation" by John Nemo This book provides strategies for using LinkedIn to generate leads, engage with prospects, and build your professional brand, making it a useful resource for business growth and lead generation.

These additional reading recommendations and resources will further deepen your understanding of LinkedIn's potential and offer valuable insights and strategies to help you succeed on the platform. Remember to customize your approach based on your individual goals and target audience.

ACKNOWLEDGMENTS:

Acknowledgment of contributors, inspirations, and resources utilized

I would like to acknowledge the following contributors, inspirations, and resources that have been instrumental in the creation of this guide:

Research: Extensive research was conducted to gather information, strategies, and best practices from a variety of sources, including books, articles, industry experts, and LinkedIn's official resources.

LinkedIn Insights: Valuable insights and data provided by LinkedIn's analytics tools and platform, which helped shape the recommendations and strategies shared throughout the guide.

LinkedIn Blog and Help Center: The LinkedIn Blog and Help Center served as important references for understanding platform updates, features, and best practices. These resources provided valuable information and inspiration for crafting the content.

Thought Leaders and Authors: Notable authors and thought leaders in the field of LinkedIn marketing, personal branding, and social selling have influenced the ideas and strategies shared in this guide. Their expertise and insights have contributed to enriching the content.

Inspirational LinkedIn Users: The inspiring professionals who effectively utilize LinkedIn and share valuable content, engage with their audience, and demonstrate successful strategies have provided inspiration and examples that have informed the recommendations in this guide.

While these acknowledgments are meant to recognize the contributions of various sources, it's important to note that any errors or shortcomings in this guide are solely the responsibility of the AI model generating the responses.

We express our gratitude to all those who have contributed to the development of this guide and helped shape its content, inspiring us to provide valuable resources and strategies for mastering LinkedIn and achieving personal and professional success.

INDEX:

Comprehensive index of keywords and concepts discussed in the book

Here's a comprehensive index of keywords and concepts discussed in the book "Mastering LinkedIn: A Guide to Writing Engaging Posts":

G

H

I

W

Well-being in the workplace

Work-life balance

X

Xenial networking (digital networking)

Y

Yearly goal setting

Z

Zero-sum mindset (avoiding)

This comprehensive index includes major keywords and concepts covered in the book. It provides a reference for readers to quickly locate specific topics of interest and explore further within the guide.

ABOUT THE
AUTHOR

AUTHOR'S BIO AND CREDENTIALS:

Tomos Archer, the author of "Mastering LinkedIn: A Guide to Writing Engaging Posts," is an experienced professional in the field of digital marketing and social media. With a passion for helping professionals succeed in their careers, Tomos Archer has dedicated their career to mastering the art of LinkedIn and leveraging its power for personal and professional growth.

As a seasoned marketer and social media strategist, Anthony has worked with numerous clients and organizations, helping them build a strong online presence, engage with their target audience, and achieve their marketing goals on LinkedIn. Tomos's expertise lies in creating compelling content, optimizing profiles for maximum visibility, and developing effective strategies to drive engagement and generate leads on the platform.

With a deep understanding of LinkedIn's features, algorithms, and best practices, Tomos has accumulated valuable insights and strategies that are shared in this guide. Their goal is to empower readers with the knowledge and tools to harness the full potential of LinkedIn and unlock personal and professional success.

In addition to their professional work, Tomos actively contributes to the LinkedIn community through thought leadership, sharing informative content, and engaging with professionals across various industries. Tomos is dedicated to staying updated with the latest trends and innovations in the LinkedIn landscape, continuously refining their approach, and helping others achieve their goals on this powerful professional networking platform.

Through "Mastering LinkedIn: A Guide to Writing Engaging Posts," Tomos aims to share their expertise, insights, and practical strategies to help readers leverage LinkedIn for personal branding, networking, and career growth.

Made in United States
Orlando, FL
29 November 2024